Roses In My Mind

collection of poetry

Srina Bose

First Published in July 2021

ISBN: 978-93-5427-935-5

BLUEROSE PUBLISHERS

www.bluerosepublishers.com

info@bluerosepublishers.com

+91 8882 898 898

Cover Design:

Priyanca Singh

Typographic Design:

Tanya Raj Upadhyay

Distributed by: BlueRose, Amazon, Flipkart

Table of Contents

Love

and her poisoned thorns

The Tragedy of Love

I didn't wake up and know,
I didn't have each vein running through my hand,
And each breath of air,
Tell me,
That I was in love.

It came slowly,
Spreading like a disease.
The poems that spilt out,
When I said his name,
And the roses that bloomed,
When he held my hand.

It spread like a wave,
Brushing upon my shores,
Each grain on my body,
And each wilting rose that danced on my sheath.

It didn't happen fast,
It didn't happen in the glint of a star,
Or the blink of an eye.
It happened amidst the smoke,
Of all the little fires we never noticed.

The inside jokes we'd crack,
How I'd pause the movie when he'd go get popcorn,
And be willing to share the aux cable on car rides,
Knowing that he spoke through the music he played,
And the words he never said.

It didn't happen at first sight either,
For the naked eye could never see through the masks he wore.
It could never see the words engraved on his wrists,
The reasons why his smile had always been strained,
Why he felt having a favourite colour was mean,
And that coffee with milk was the epitome of disaster,
That the world was a shallow void of suffering,
And also,
How Five Star was much better than Dairy Milk.

The ordinary eye,
Could never see the beauty within him.

It happened slowly,
With each burden he unloaded,
Each shield he shed,
And each second that passed,

Where no Pink Floyd, or Nirvana,
Could replicate my favourite music,
Which was the harmony of his breaths on my neck.

It didn't happen fast,
It spread slowly,
Like a moth spreading its wings across your heart.

It didn't happen fast,
For the tragedy of love,
Never does.

~Srina

Yesterday, I Dreamt of You

Yesterday, I dreamt of silver lights,
Lined up on my arm,
Flickering with the cadence of your breaths.
I dreamt of the streetlights we sat under,
When your car broke down,
Under which your hair glowed,
And your eyes glimmered,
And I forgot about the darkness towering over us.

I dreamt of the day,
You traced my skin,
To find my wounds,
Completing the half-inflicted ones on yours.
I dreamt of the day we lay under the sun,
The emerald grass hugging your hair,
And dew-drops settling onto your ear lobe,
And how,
When you smiled,
The world seemed to as well.

I dreamt of the night you held me,
Picking up my broken pieces,
And holding them in your arms.
I dreamt of those Sunday mornings
With marmalade on toast.
And how I'd always burn the bread,

But you'd never mind.
And for a fleeting moment,
It reminded me of myself.
Burnt,
And charred to the brim.
Yet,
You still stayed,
You still woke up next to me,
You still held me all those nights I bled silver.

Yesterday,
I dreamt of silver lights,
Lighting up,
All the nights,
We saw each other bleed.

Yesterday,
I dreamt of you,
And all the highways I'd ride across,
To always come back to you.

~*Srina*

You are Music

I carry an empty violin case across my back,
To remind myself,
How the music I once played,
Will never sound the same again.
The violin within it is empty,
Empty like an artist,
Without inspiration;
And a poet—
Without words.

I pluck a string,
To make a sound,
A sound that makes itself heard,
Yet not enough,
For it to be called music.

For I wouldn't call something deprived of love,
And deprived of a person to play for—
Music.
I wouldn't call a soulless melody,
And a heartless chorus,
One without that someone,
To hold the violin for,
And stroke the bow for,
Music.
I wouldn't call the hollow abyss in the sound I
make, music.

It's like a vase,
Painted with the best paints,
But left abandoned,
Without the flowers it deserves.

I don't call the music I make without you,
Music.
I call it a sound.
A sound of loneliness,
And desolation.
A sound of silent breathing,
Against the pillow I press my forehead on,
A sound of hushed tears that permeate through my skin,
A sound of waking up everyday,
To find myself,
In the same desert I gave up in yesterday.
A sound of silent desire,
Desire for the drumbeat of your company,
Or the harmony of your breaths,
I'm not quite sure.

But all I know,
Is that it's not music.
That the music I make without you,
Can't be called music.

~Srina

Broken Love; Broken Poetry

i. Sometimes I talk to my poems,
They're a friend to me, you see,
They hear me,
Through the words I write,
They know me,
Through the ink I bleed,
Yet, they never talk back.

ii. I request my poems,
Not to weave themselves around you.
To not let your fragrance infiltrate,
Through the coffee stained pages.
To not remind me,
Of the broken wine glasses we once drank from,
The Sunday mornings we spent,
With my head resting on your chest.
As I don't want to make my poems a memorial of our love,
Yet, I'm writing one right now.

iii. When you hurt me,
My poems came out better,
But when you loved me,
I never wrote poems,
As words can't describe it.
Simple lines,

Joined by an aching hand,
Can't describe love.
They can't describe you.

iv. How much of blood, tears and aching hearts, does it take,
To turn a love poem into an eulogy;
The pages into a coffin,
And the words—
Simply decaying skeletons,
Wishing to see the sun one last time.

v. My poems never speak,
Yet they are heard by the people who read them,
You were like that for me.
You heard me,
Until the words in our destiny turned black,
Until the bones we hugged,
Turned to dust.
You loved me,
Until the pages of our eulogy were read out,
Until every graveyard,
Waiting for the corpses of our love, were dug,
Until, every poem was torn apart.
Until, we were out of love.

~*Srina*

I Broke the Vase

I broke the vase,
It slipped out of my hand,
And dropped,
With the grace of a dancer,
With worn out legs.

I broke the vase,
It dropped through my fingers,
As if it had been waiting to,
Since the day you gifted it to me.

The delicate glass pieces shattered,
Onto the ground,
And a puzzle of a million strands,
Before my eyes,
Were carefully laid out.

My hand trembled as I brushed my finger,
Against the serrated edges.
The relics of our decaying love,
Sharp, and frustrated—piercing through my skin.

I dropped the vase.
The vase in which I'd kept the first flower you
gave me,
And the last fragment of the affection you
breathed.

The flowers have no home now,
Yes—there are a million other vases,
Stacked away in attics I'll never visit;
But none of them are *your* vase,
The one *I* broke.
The flowers can't live there,
Under the roof of an unknown entity;
For love seeks a home,
Not a shelter.

I broke the vase.
And even if I try to fix it,
With the plaster of another meager lover,
The edges will still stay bare,
And the abyss of my faults,
Still visible from the corner of my eyes.

I broke the vase.
The one that preserved our love,
And cradled it each night,
While singing a lullaby,
With the melody of our lies.
I broke the vase.
And now the flowers that grew in it,
And the love that slept beneath its shade—
They,
Are broken too.

~Srina

Finding You in Myself

i. How broken do you have to be,
To stay at the crime scene,
To lie motionless,
Feel the blood drain out of your wrists,
Wrap the caution tape,
Around your flaking skin,
Drape curtains against the scars on your body,
Make peace with death,
And love with darkness.

ii. You asked me once,
"Can you break something enough,
To turn it to dust?"
I showed you my body.

iii. I was crying broken pearls;
Yet you saw wings being weaved.

iv. My neck bends into your body,
Bending for you,
Breaking into three pieces;
Love,
Disease,
And the revival you breathe into me.

v. Sweaters on my body,
Slowly slipping off,
Within your golden arms.
I smile,
But you can't tell in the darkness.
You trace my collarbones,
And whisper that they're like the shore,
In a dark somber ocean,
And I hurt a milli-particle less.

vi. You gave me a bouquet once,
I threw it away,
As I toss away the things that love me,
Into a bin of things I tell myself I don't deserve.
Sometimes I see those flowers in your eyes,
On your fingertips,
The iris that glistens when you smile,
And the cupids above your lips.
Sunflowers in your eyes,
Roses in your smile,
And thorns from all the dead flowers I birthed,
Joined in a broken chain around your neck.

vii. I smell silver on your skin.
The colour.

It reminds me of cigarettes,
And vodka bottles shattering,
And us,
Burning in the night sky,
Charred at every crevice,
But beautiful.
That's what we were,
Painfully beautiful.

~Srina

Love Letters I Never Gave

i. I can't help but notice,
The finger-prints on your neck.
They're like tire marks on an abandoned road,
A road which they use,
To get where they want,
But then, never return.
Whose are they?
I ask you,
But your roads are dying,
And my voice fails to reach you.
Who did you take home?
When I wasn't there to give you a ride.
But your roads are dying,
And my voice dies with them.

ii. You hold a cigarette in your hand;
A cloud of smoke, hugging your face,
And ash floating off your hair.
"Can I sing you a love song?"
I ask,
But you don't reply.
"Drunk people are already in love with the night,"
You then say,
And I fold the poem I wrote for you,

And the song I wished to sing,
Back into the pocket full of art,
Which can’t bring out the beauty,
I witness every day.

iii. I can't help but notice,
How you wear your wounds like a trophy.
How you're the first girl who doesn't hide them,
Who displays it in the glass closet of their skin,
Exhibited for all the people who gave them,
To remind them,
How a little blood never ruined true beauty.

iv. Sometimes I watch the silver chains you wear.
You had once said,
Each bead signifies a sin in your life,
The first: birth,
And the last: me.
But from the corner of my eyes,
And the hooks of your neck,
I know,
Those aren’t silver chains.
They're bruises, pretending to be chains.

v. I see your skin flaking away,
After each drink you sip,
And each relic of a cigarette you breathe.
The paper melting,
And the words that once spelt 'beauty',
Dissolving into a new you—
Into someone unfamiliar to my touch.

vi. My arms tremble when they touch you,
My finger-tips marking their grief onto you.
They're tomb stones on the cemetery your body has become,
They're dew drops on a dying plant,
They're the 'SOS' sign we trace on sand,
Only to be swept away by the passing waves.
They're seeds of love;
On a decaying garden,
An oasis in the desert your heart has become.
My hands on you,
Are roses for a dying soul,
You tell me,
As you slip out of my reach,
Slowly fading from my pupils,
Burying under the heap of flowers I wish I had given you,
And the pile of poetry I wish I had read.

"Roses for a dying soul",
You repeat.

vii. Are you dying?
I ask,
But dead people never reply.

~Srina

A Lover Isn't Enough

That night,
I wish he had called me,
And I wish he had told me.

I wish he hadn't been alone on the terrace,
Alone,
While counting his breaths,
Alone,
While walking towards the railing,
And alone,
With his legs dangling off,
And his eyes shut,
Watching the ground beneath him,
Breathe this name.

He could have left one message,
Just one text,
One little ping on my phone,
And I'd have seen it,
I'd have already snatched the keys,
And have started the car.

He could have called me,
Just once,
He knows I would have picked up.
I'd hear the tremble in his voice,

And I'd know,
I'd know what he was about to do.

I'd drive down,
Drive down the coffee shop we had our first date,
When he offered to pay,
But had forgotten his wallet at home.

I'd see the gym he promised to go every morning,
But gave up on after two days.
The grocery shop,
Where he broke a peanut butter jar,
And I couldn't stop laughing about it for a week.

I'd drive past the mall,
The lift in which he slipped his hand in mine,
And traced my palm,
With all the words he never got the chance to say.

I'd drive past the park,
Where we had our first major fight,
And he refused to talk to me for a day,
But pretence hatred never lasted last long.

We sat on the swings the next day and I bought him Butterscoth icecream,
Only I knew, he hated every other flavour.
And I'd think after tonight would be over,
And he'd be safe and sound,

Away from that terrace,
I'll buy him some ice cream tomorrow.

Tomorrow was three years ago.

I'd drive past the movie theatre,
Where we watched this one terrible film,
And both fell asleep,
Onto each other's shoulders,
And that feeling was better than any movie we could have watched.

But none of this happened,
As I stayed at home,
Watched dawn break,
And he never called me.

Even after having my phone number saved on his favourite contacts,
And our photo set as his phone wallpaper,
Even after the days we spent sewing back,
The tapestries on each other's skin,
And drew stars on each other's scars,
And traced our future onto the midnight sky—
Even after all this,
He never called.

It's tragic,
How despite all the life we gave birth to,
He still chose death.

Maybe the voices never really go.
Maybe you really can't fill a void of emptiness with even more of it.
Maybe love isn't enough.
Maybe I,
Was not enough.
Maybe a call,
A simple text,
A note,
That said why he did what he did,
That explained how he was leaving,
Not me,
But the world we built,
That grew in the palms of our hands,
Throbbing and pulsing until he let go of the railing,
Until he left.

Maybe a mere lover,
Isn't enough,
To shut out the voices in your head.

Maybe a mere lover,
Isn't enough,
To want to live.

~*Srina*

I Still Have Your Rose

I still have your rose,
The one you gave me last summer,
I clench it in my wrist,
And press it against my chest.
The petals have fallen off,
And the stem is frail and gray,
But I've still not throw it away.
I still keep it,
Carefully in my drawer,
Each day watching it,
As I move on.

I can't go back to you,
You've hurt me too much,
But I can always go back to the rose,
Hold it tight within my aching hands,
Watch the withering petals,
Each a sign,
That even without you,
My roots can grow,
That even without your love,
My roses can bloom,
That even after you're gone,
I still have a token,
Of the shallow gifts you gave,
The hearts you broke,

And the roses,
That bloomed,
Only once you left.

~Srina

Disease

and her eternal scars

Blood Tastes Like Honey

Beads of red,
That find their home,
On the cracks of my lips.
And dewdrops of agony,
That travel through my skin,
Settling where you dig your nails.

It tastes like honey,
But it isn't golden.
It's red;
The stain of red,
That covers the pavement,
Painted with the blood,
Of someone we love,
Yet,
You never loved me.

This is honey,
The honey,
We spread on the bread,
And have for a sweet little breakfast,
With an Abba cassette playing at the back.
It's what comes to mind,
When you think of 'home'.
But the honey I bleed,
The honey I weave with my peeling skin,

It isn't sweet.
It's pain.

The pain, I've now made a friend,
The pain I welcome,
When I rip the band aids off my skin,
The pain that comes back to me,
Like a magnet finding its unlike pole.
The pain of the tears,
That sting my cheeks,
The pain that wraps itself around me,
When you press against my body,
Tearing off my hair,
And ripping off the very skin I wear,
The honey basked skin,
That you seem to love each night.

It tastes like the midnight sun,
That follows me,
When I wish to sleep,
The way you do.
Crawling up on my bed,
Your hand, discreetly slipping within my dress,
When I wish to be left alone.
Engraving your handprints,
On my skin,
When I wish to be untouched.

It tastes like the current.
When we touch a loose wire,
That holds onto us,
Until we burn,
Until one of us is gone first,
But I'm always the first to go,
It's never you.

The blood I bleed tastes like honey.
The honey,
In which I drown,
In which I bathe,
Which I've made my home,
My shelter,
My everything.
Yet,
1 wonder why,
This honey,
Is never sweet.

~Srina

Afraid of Falling

I've always been,
Afraid of falling;
So afraid,
That I lived my life,
Caged;
And with my hands cuffed,
Within the void of my own prickling comfort.

I've always been,
Afraid of falling;
So afraid,
That I could never release,
The chains,
That clung onto my potential,
So afraid—
That the same chains,
Engulfed it all.

I've always been,
Afraid of falling;
So afraid,
That I never learnt,
What it was like,
To stand through the storm,
To withstand the wind,
Which pushes us aside.

So afraid—
That I never learnt how to stand up again.

I've always been,
Afraid of falling;
Falling into the endless pit,
Called love;
So afraid—
That I never found the person,
To hold onto,
When I fell through the cracks of life.

I've always been,
Afraid of falling,
More afraid, of not being able to,
Pick up my fallen pieces;
So afraid—
That I had broken into pieces,
And fallen,
While standing, all along.

~*Srina*

Unerasable Beauty

Why is it that every time I pass by a mirror,
I avoid the reflection looking at me,
As if ashamed of the stranger,
Judging my scars.

Why is it that the Instagram filters,
Have now become a part of my identity,
Clinging onto my skin,
And comforting my pleading insecurity.

Why is it that even with so much makeup on,
My face still feels bare-naked,
Deprived of the tint of reality,
That no contour or eye shadow can bring.

Why is it that I despise makeup removers,
As they pull apart the curtain,
Between the face I'm used to hating,
And the mask, I pretend to like.

Every night, when I wash my face,
I see the skin I no longer recognise,
And the darkness of my complexion,
That I hide every day, with bad editing and
photoshop.

I look at the stranger in the mirror,
And a voice inside of me says,
A voice I shut down,
Every time I look at myself.
The voice whispers to me,
That maybe underneath,
All those unnecessary filters,
Still remains,
A spark of beauty,
No insecurity can erase.

~*Srina*

Poems For Her

i. I admire her yet hate her at the same time,
It's maddening.
I hate looking at her,
For she's everything I'm insecure about,
Yet I sneak glances,
To see what really is,
That I despise her for.

ii. She cries a lot,
Holding handkerchiefs engraved with tears,
And the reasons behind them.
One of them has my name engraved.

iii. I'd like to hold her sometimes.
Just for a fleeting moment.
I want to hold her hand;
The nails,
From which she carves herself.
The glistening iris,
Which refuses to see the light she emits,
And the eyelashes,
Woven with the cloth she spun,
From spending nights crying herself to sleep,

But she’s so surreal.
A shadow of all the good things,
And a reflection of all the flaws.
Awfully blurred,
Unseen during night,
And concealed behind glass during day.
She looks at me,
And I see her eyes reflecting the beauty,
Invisible to both of us,
For, we are one.

iv. I move forward,
And whisper to the broken glass,
"Why can't I love you?"
And sob as the mirror slips through my hands,
As each particle that told me and the mirror I hold,
To leave this world forever,
Evaporates.
While each pore I was born to hate,
Disappears.
While I forget how much I hated this very mirror,
And the girl that sobbed in it.

~Srina

My Anxiety

She has always been a strange woman,
Residing everywhere I go,
Each corner of my home,
And each crevice of my skin.
She creeps up on my arms,
Like unwanted wines,
And takes hold of me,
Until her dead flowers are all that bloom on me.

She lies in my trembling hands when I turn the steering wheel,
The beads of sweat that drip down when I stand in an elevator,
The pang in my chest when I'm surrounded by people I don't know.

She lies in the carcasses of each thought within me,
And in each temporary joy I seize.

She is a strange woman,
To suppress whom I have taken so many pills,
Yet she is never satisfied.
She is greedy,
Always begging for more,

She begs for each joy I gain,
And wants to bleed onto it.

She begs for each thought I have,
And wishes to make them her own.
She begs for my body,
And wishes to make it a womb,
To birth only her darkness.

She always wants more of me,
And so,
I give in.

But she's one wicked woman,
Who enjoys flowing out of my pain,
She enjoys rubbing salt in my wounds,
She enjoys being the reason behind my tears,
She enjoys being the trigger behind all my
gunshots,
And the ghost writer of all my eulogies.

She follows me,
And I can't push her off,
As her kiss bleeds a drug onto me,
A drug the pills I take, can't replicate.

It's strange, it really is,
How she is the one who breaks me,
Carefully slicing me into wounds that can clot on her wrists,
She is the one who ruins me,
And kills me over and over again,
Yet the only one who stays behind,
And sings me to sleep,
With a lullaby on how I should save my tears,
As there is more blood to bleed,
More tears to weave,
And more nights to grieve.

That's the woman who is always beside me,
My wretched and forlorn anxiety.

~Srina

2:41 A.M.

I check my watch,
It's 2:41 a.m.,
I hear it ticking across my wrist,
Spinning through the time I've spent drinking,
With beads of glass spilling out of my mouth,
And your name pulsing in each crevice of my skin.

I'm in the bathroom,
My heart thuds against the cigarettes around my ribs,
And I watch my reflection;
A museum of scars,
And clunks of flesh that sculpt me,
Into the person you always wanted me to be.

It's 2:41 a.m.,
The moon is blossoming,
And the night sways to the music.
Another beer bottle is being opened,
Another heart being crushed,
And another star bleeding out of my lips.

It's 2:41 a.m.,
And I see you,
Dancing against the bar,
With your hands laced around the vodka bottles,

You threw at my face.
I point at the scar on my forehead,
But you're drunk,
And drunk people never look back at what they once broke.

I see the ash tray you shattered,
On our second anniversary,
The curtain you ripped apart,
The day before my birthday,
The rancor in your nails,
When you held my hair between your fingers,
Blood stained and aching with malice,
Yet you called it,
Love.

I see you,
On the tip of my tongue,
As I chug another drink,
The last one,
I tell myself,
Just like the way you did,
Before you did what you did to me.
It's 2:41 a.m.,
The night lies at its deathbed,
While dawn caresses it to sleep,
And I watch the moon drown into your hair.

It's 2:41 a.m.,
And I count the lasts I've promised to myself.
Each one,
Too ancient.

It's 2:41 a.m.,
And I taste you,
In the red wine flowing through my throat,
Dripping down my veins like IV.

It's 2:41 a.m.,
And I think I have bled enough for a night.
I take another puff,
And you come closer,
To hold me under the collapsing skies,
And trace my lips with venom,
'This is the last time',
You whisper,
And the wine turns bitter with our lies.
And my watch turns one minute closer to dawn.

~Srina

Strangers I Have Known

i. There was this one boy I met at a Science competition,
It was at a different school, a different world,
Yet I remember him.
His maroon coloured uniform and curly hair,
And a smile which was the kind you'd want to wake up to.
I remember he was listening to Pink Floyd on his earphones,
But out loud and unaware that we could hear.
I poked his shoulder and said,
"We can hear it,"
And he replied with a grin,
"That's the intention."

I remember wanting to ask him his name,
He seemed like an 'Aditya' kind of person,
But I never was the one to speak up.

Then, we talked,
He told me how he forgot his presentation midway but still got second position,
He told me his favourite Pink Floyd song (I obviously guessed it),
And why he thought they were the best band to exist,
He also told me how he had always liked arts but was forced to take science by his parents,
And also how the refreshments at this school tasted bad.

We talked a lot,
All throughout the boring speeches and presentations,
We exchanged little anecdotes,
Little things that I still remember,
Yet we never shared our names.

ii. There was this librarian I knew,
She'd always smile at me when I'd enter the hall.
She knew me better than all my friends combined,
Only by my book choices.
She knew how young adult fiction made me puke,

And how gruesome thrillers were what kept me awake at night,
She knew how I preferred soft covers over hard ones,
And loved reading the author's notes.
She was the mother to some of my favourite books.

But one day she didn't turn up for work.
The attachment you end up feeling for a stranger is odd,
It is the attachment you never notice,
Until the person leaves.

But I didn't question anything,
And moved on with life,
Flicked another page and moved onto another chapter,
Yet at the back of my mind,
Every time I start reading a new book,
I wish I'd have asked that sweet librarian who had a mole on her left cheek,
And a smile traced with delicate wrinkles—
I wish I'd have asked her,
Her name.

iii. There was this one girl I met online,
Like me, she was broken—
A poet.
She went by a pen name and so did I,
She'd comment on my posts and so did I on hers,
We knew each other not by the masks we held,
But the words we bled.

Now that I think of it,
It was beautiful.
The way we knew nothing about each other,
No name, city or age,
Yet knew each other better than anyone else,
As our poems carried the truth we held.

But one day,
As I searched her up to see if she wrote anything new,
Her account was gone.
Disabled, or deleted,
I'll never know,
But it had disappeared,
And I never got the chance to read more of her works,

Nor the chance to know more than the page she wrote on,
And even today,
As I bleed out another poem,
My hands still ache at the thought,
That I will never know the name,
Of that one stranger on the internet,
Who was more caring,
Than anyone I have ever known.
Messaging me her thoughts about my work,
No names or personal details,
But just a conversation between two artists,
Trying to find their way.

This one stranger was there for me,
When no real life person could be.

~Srina

Ghosts Don't Scare Me

Ma,
I'm not the same person anymore.
The same person,
Who'd scream during horror movies,
Who'd force her eyes shut,
When someone raised their hand.
Not the same person,
Who'd cover her ears,
When the cacophony of the spirits would start—
The spirits in my bed,
Who you said didn't exist,
Yet, slept with me each night.

No, Ma,
The edges of stray knives,
Don't scare me anymore,
For they are my friends now,
And their touch,
A kiss no lover can plant.

No, Ma,
A prick from a nail,
And a drop of blood,
Like the bindi you wear—
Don't make me cry anymore.

No, Ma,
I don't want you to leave the lights on,
During nights when the darkness feels too close;
As maybe my eyes seek a companion.
A companion that the darkness seems to be.

No, Ma,
You don't have to give me band-aids,
For the mysterious wounds that appear,
As their very purpose,
Is for me to have something to suffer from.
And how do I tell you, Ma?
I'm not scared of ghosts,
I'm scared of people.

After all I've seen;
Broken glass,
Disarranged lies,
And a catacomb of skeletons,
That I hide in my closet;
After all this—
Ghosts don't scare me, Ma,
For friends aren't supposed to be scary.
They're supposed to hold your hand,
And sing you to sleep,
The way you used to, Ma.

Ghosts don't suck out the glint of joy,
That lived within the eyes of their friends,
From the people,
They had told "I'll be there for you",
Yet have their hand,
Discreetly wrapped around the dagger across their back.

No Ma,
Ghosts don't betray,
People do.
Ghosts don't kill,
People do.

Ghosts don't scare me anymore,
As they reside everywhere I go,
In the diary you read secretly each night,
The rooms I lock tight.
They even live in your eyes, Ma.
The ghosts that linger on my arm,
Tracing the wounds,
That you know who gave—
Those ghosts don't scare me anymore,
The people who inflicted those wounds, do.
Ghosts don't scare me anymore, Ma,
You do.

The people around me,
Who keep daggers within their pockets,
Like toffees to offer,
They do.
Ghosts don't scare me anymore, Ma,
People do.

~Srina

The Storm Lasted Too Long

i. It's a little sad,
How the flames that hug me,
And the prison that kills me,
Is the only home I have,
And the death I witness each day,
My only family.

ii. I'd rather be charred to the brim,
And have my skin peeling off,
Than come out clean,
For my scars are what give meaning to my life now,
And the flames burn not me,
But the grief stained across my skin,
And without them—
I have nothing.

iii. It's sad how the horizons change,
What once was the kiss between the heavens and the ground,
Is now my ceiling,
And the walls that encapsulate the storms,
My only sky.

iv. I watch the furnace,
And the pyre of each moment of my life,
I have killed.
I watch my hands melt to dust,
When I try to reach for the horizon,
And my chest seeking comfort,
Only in the eye of the storm.

The smoke has sang to me for so long,
That I've forgotten,
The breath of air,
And the taste of life.
I've danced in the storms for so long,
That I've forgotten,
The blue sky,
One without the blood stained rays of the sun.

v. I write my sorrows,
Each little one in a diary,
Each word blooming into a rose,
Only to die when they receive the sunlight given by my sun,
For it isn't light,
It's bloodshed.
As when you try so hard to find the light amongst the darkness,
You're ready to pretend the blood is light,

You're ready to believe the light never even existed,
That the pain had always been your life,
And that death is what breathes life into you.

vi. I didn't think the storm would last so long,
So long that the eye of the cyclone,
Is all I'd ever see,
So long,
That the very prison that chokes me,
Is what'll come to mind,
When I think of,
'Home'.

~Srina

Revival

and all the light she gave

Little Fires You Left Behind

I remember that day,
Wearing those tight jeans,
That felt like metal around my waist,
Beads of sweat dripping down my thigh;
And that pink rubber band,
Which always slipped off my hair.

I remember the sun,
Glaring into my eyes,
Not the kind,
That made your hair glisten,
And your face beam,
But the kind which stares at you,
Wanting you to see,
Everything you turned a blind eye to.

It's like fires in the sky,
Little fires, you left behind.

I remember soaked cheeks,
Whose were they, I can't recall.
But they were infiltrated with tears,
Tears from all the little fires we never noticed.

I remember music,
Not Mumford and Sons,

Or Pink Floyd,
Not the cd's you played on every occasion,
Or the 94.3 radio channel,
You switched onto every car ride.
They were beeps,
Of the monotonous ventilators,

And death.
Death's somber voice,
Which you can only hear,
When it's near someone you love.

I remember suffocating.
Inside the hospital walls,
Inside those denim jeans,
Holding my breath,
As if one breath I take,
Is equal to one purloined from you.

I remember holding your hand,
But it wasn't skin,
It was metal.
Metal bars,
Of the hospital bed,
In which you lay.
With death stroking your hair,
You reunited with your worst enemy on that bed.

I remember tiles.
Tiles whose patterns I can draw by heart.
Circles, and triangles,
Intersected by lines,
Lines drawn by you,
And that day,
That have clung onto me,
Kissing me, holding me,
And suffocating me,
Like those goddamn denim jeans.

I remember things I shouldn't,
Things I curse myself to forget,
Things I wish would evaporate into the sky,
But they stay.

But most of all,
I remember you,
And all the light you gave,
Which throbbed,
Until your last breath,
Beating and fluttering,
And then,
Left,
With the blink of an eye,
The flick of a finger,
And the beep of a ventilator.

I remember sunlight amidst the darkness,
And darkness amidst the sunlight,
And death among a million hearts,
And a million little fires everywhere.

I remember looking at the ground,
And noticing one footstep less,
But also looking at the heavens above,
And seeing one star more.

~Srina

Griefcase

It happened after that day,
After 26th December 2012,
How she became a traveller.

She started carrying a griefcase everywhere she'd go.
It had no clothes or objects,
But was simply an empty box,
Holding the memories of the little girl that was once hers,
But now, just another story left incomplete.

She thinks of the day Sanya, her daughter, took her first steps,
In those pink squeaky shoes,
Walking over the grey tiles,
And she waited with a camera in her hand,
But before she could take a video,
Sanya had already fallen onto the ground.
But a part of her was grateful,
As the best memories can never be preserved in a piece of metal,
Only the mind,
And the brief cases a mother carries,
Can hold them together.

She thinks of Sanya's favourite colour,
Pink.
How she insisted that her room be only pink.
Now she realises,
That the griefcase with the remains of her daughter,
Is pink as well.

She thinks of her second birthday,
How her husband had already left,
And this house had become a sanctuary,
Of two lonely girls trying to keep each other's company.

She thinks of her first day of school,
The uniform that she had carefully ironed,
But Sanya had come home with it completely dirty,
And spilt red paint on it.
She thinks of how it symbolised the night of 26th December 2012,
And how, the blood woven around that day,
Was already predicted on her first day in school.

She thinks of the night of 26th September 2012,
Sanya's 18th birthday,
How she never came home,
But a week later,
A body,

An autopsy report,
And a pink griefcase came.

She doesn't want to know what happened,
She wants to shut out the voices,
Which said that Sanya was drunk and driving,
How she ran into another car,
And how,
Her Ma,
Who did everything a woman was painted not to do,
Worked for her, earned for her, and lived for her—
Never saw her little daughter become an adult,
She never got a gift from her first salary,
She never got to meet her future husband,
To grow frail and old and have a picture of all the life she birthed,
Hanging on the wall behind her fridge,
And mark the birthdays of all her grandchildren's on her calendar,
And prepare her famous chilly chicken just for them.

Sometimes the stale smell of death,
Replaces all the life it purloined,
And now,
Even after years of it,
The smell still lingers,

The cold and clammy hands from that night still hug her,
And each day she still cries in Sanya's bedroom,
As if her tears can build up, drop by drop,
The person Sanya once was.
But she knows that no matter what she does,
The memories of all the light that was purloined,
In the pink griefcase,
Is all that remains.

~*Srina*

Colours

Blue is the colour of the sky,
The sky I'd colour as a child,
Scribbling with those Faber Castell crayons,
Held between my tender fingers.

Blue is also the colour of the ink,
The ink through which I've wept,
I've screamed,
I've cried,
And have been heard by all the skies.

Red is the colour of the heart I drew,
In which I wrote his name.
The heart I drew at the back of every notebook,
And on top of every secret diary.

Red is also the colour of the blood,
The blood I bleed, yet don't show.
The pain.
The anguish;
The flowing sorrows,
Kept carefully within the vessels of deception.

Black is the colour of the dress I wanted,
Draped over the clothing racks,

In stores I could never afford,
And on models I could never look like.

Black is also the coffee I drink,
And the lonely nights I have spent,
Gazing at the stars,
And breathing in the solitude.

Pink is the colour of the bracelet he gave me,
That I still have in my drawer,
It's the colour of the birthday card he bought,
Where he wrote a poem that's etched onto my heart.

Pink is also the merlot I drink every weekend,
Dripping down my veins like IV,
As I try to forget how he is not mine anymore.

These colours bleed into each other,
Spreading onto the palette of our life,
And drenching themselves,
In the brush strokes of today.

The paintings I painted before,
Don't feel the same now,
And the colours of today look so lovely,
But by each passing day,
The shades change.

The past gets duller,
Fading away into the barren canvases of yesterday,
And the present brightens,
Dancing and leaping,
Through the glistening today,
Making its way, to the luminescent tomorrow.

The colours don't look the same,
They never will,
As I'm growing,
My roots are being watered,
And the body I was taught to hate,
Is being loved.
And I realize now,

I'm loved,
And so is this world,
And I am making another painting,
Writing another story,
And the colours of today,
All the blood I've bled,
And the art I have woven,
They have never been more beautiful.

~Srina

The Old Grey Banyan Tree

If I were to go there now,
Blindfolded and deprived of his beauty,
I'd still know exactly where he lies,
As the path is alive in my memories.

I remember each and every moment, vividly,
How we'd jump out of our classrooms when the bell would ring,
And run towards him,
And the stone benches, beside him,
In which we'd play, laugh and grow.

The ground underneath my feet,
Would be familiar and friendly.
Each rock and each pebble,
Carefully imprinted within me.

I'd walk over to the old grey Banyan tree,
And trace my fingers, over his bark,
The rough and jagged edges,
There to remind me of all the years he had been there.
Of all the children,
He had spent his afternoons with,
And all the evenings,
He had spent beneath the glowing sky.
If I could go there now,

I would.
It would be like a reunion with an old friend,
I'd catch up, while resting my feet on the ground,
Feel the dried leaves, rustle beneath me,
And the ants crawl up my skin.

We were taught as kids,
About the roots of a tree,
How the Banyan, was unique,
Having roots which we could see—
Aerial roots.
That made me admire the majestic tree even more.
How he was willing to show us his roots,
His very origin and his end,
How he embraced every inch of his body,
The charred trunk and the cracked twigs,
All with a certain sense of pride.

I'd sit, beneath the shade,
With the golden hour, glazing on my skin,
And I'd count the leaves,
The leaves that are yet to fall,
And brave enough to live,
And I'd count the years,
The years after which,
I've come to meet,
The forgotten, old grey Banyan tree.

~*Srina*

Parasite

There they stand,
Clutching the only traces,
That hold them from starvation.

Plastic toys,
That no one cares to buy.
And cheap magnets,
They can't get to sell.

Isn't it sad?
How they have made,
The streets their shelter,
And the sky,
Their roof.
The jagged roads,
With tyre marks,
Of cars they can never afford,
Are their home.
And the poverty that they accept,
Like a firefly accepting death,
Is the blanket,
They wrap around every night.

I see the charred skin,
That hangs onto their bones,
The bones that die bit by bit,
Each day.

Each fabric,
That's draped over their body,
Is a piece from another.
The mismatched socks,
The tethered shirt,
All torn off,
From richer people,
Who wouldn't want it.

Isn't it sad?
How they are a piece of each of us,
A piece of everything we have shed,
And bled.
They carry our remains,
Yet, in our minds,
They're just a crippling parasite,
Whose very existence,
Lies in their desperation to survive.

~Srina

Why Do Fireflies Die So Young?

My backyard is a grave of all the fireflies.
Who died before seeing their own light.
You ask me,
"Why do fireflies die so young?"
But against the gush of the wind,
And the whisper of the corpses beneath my feet,
My voice goes unheard.

The sky is on fire,
Illuminated,
Like a lantern,
Held between a toddler's fingers.
You see the crevices of their skin,
From the corner of the horizon,
As fragmented clouds,
And glowing radio towers.

The sky is a wound,
I realise,
Shimmering and bleeding,
The blood clotting to form,
The cotton we weave,
And the clouds we see.

The sky is a wound,
Burning,

And hurting.
Giving off the light it breathes,
Like a sparkler on a Diwali night,
Giving and giving,
Until it's gone for good.
"The sky is a firefly",
I hear the words,
Escaping through my mouth.

In the cemetery, I preserve,
Completed with the carcasses,
Of those the world killed,
And watched die,
I wonder why,
The sky is never there.
Maybe it is because,
The sky attains peace in heaven,
Not underneath the dried grass where we played.

Yet on this grass I see the swollen shells,
And the worn out wings,
Of the fire flies who I claim to be the sky,
So which is which, you ask.
But before I can answer,
Your hand has already slipped out of mine.
And the touch of your skin,
Dried up,
And decaying,

Like the remains of all the fireflies who died before our eyes.

The wounds inflicted on the summer sky,
Are fading,
And honey, you are too.
New light is being given off.
And darling,
It feels like the bulb in my heart,
That lit up my world,
Is dying.
Dying into the darkness you left behind,
The darkness no one can replace.

New fireflies roam in the wounds above,
And new songs are being sung,
And I realise,
Now that you're gone,
You're just one of the many fireflies we witnessed,
Who died so young.

~*Srina*

Wisdom of Rain

I've always loved the rain.
How it made its presence known,
By its gentle and delicate outpour.
How it made an ordinary person,
Let go of their mundane life,
Just for a fleeting moment,
And look up,
And admire the tears of the sky,
And notice how even the strongest shed their
shields sometimes.

The rain always tells us to let go.
To let go of the vines that entangle us to our past,
And the archaic mud that clings onto our life.

As every time I trace your name,
Onto a rainy window pane,
It is always concealed,
Beneath the dripping water.

For the rain wants us to move on,
The way water does,
Flowing through each pore,
And finding its way through every crack.
The clouds want us to let go,
Of everything we pile up within,

All the words we never said,
All the tears we never shed.

I've always loved the rain,
For it reminds me,
How it is alright to cry sometimes,
And how it is alright to set yourself free.

~Srina

The Poetry of Melancholy

Gloom is a better poet than joy,
For our misery always finds a way out,
Leaping through the pen we write,
And gushing through the voice we use.

But our joy is silent.
It may appear in the glint of our smile,
Or the glimmer in our eyes,
But it's quiet.

The symphony of the joy we breathe,
Is wordless,
For our joy is not a writer.
As when I try to paint the glee I feel,
Onto the canvas of my heart,
It remains blank,
The words visible,
But the glee I tried to rebirth—
Concealed.

As happiness can't be expressed,
Within the limit of a hundred pages,
Or the space of a thousand canvases,
For our joy leaves no scars worth remembering.

Happiness doesn't dance in a pallet of paint,
It doesn't drench itself in the vulnerable ink,
It doesn't cry out to be heard,
But gloom does.

The poetry written by melancholy,
Is natural.
Flowing through the veins of her body,
Streaming out through the blood she bleeds.

Joy isn't a writer.
Joy is a show-er.
It shows you itself
Infesting upon your smile, your teeth or your eyes,
But honey,
Melancholy is a writer.
A writer,
Of the rawest form,
The purest blood.

Melancholy is a writer,
A poetess,
An author.
And the poetry of melancholy,
Is admired by joy itself.

~*Srina*

Learnings in a Democracy

Yesterday, I was strangled.
Not really,
But I was.
There are marks across my neck,
Each—a warning,
To take back the words I bled.

Yesterday,
I watched the news,
And reminded myself,
That any word, I spin wrong.
Will get me reduced to dust.

Yesterday,
I saw *lathis* and bricks,
And screams dripping with blood.
I saw newspapers torn apart,
And flags wrapped around.

Yesterday,
I saw what a democracy could be.

Yesterday,
I learnt to cover my mouth,
I learnt that each word I utter,
Has nothing but spit and lies.

I learnt to drape my head,
With worn out cloth,
And tattered flags,
And promise that my thoughts,
Shall always be beneath the country.

Yesterday,
I learnt to chug the water handed by our superiors,
Telling myself to ignore the poison—
Ignore each particle of a lie,
That builds the dagger,
We hoist every Independence Day.

Yesterday,
I learnt to doubt before I speak,
I learnt that my voice can hurt,
But still not be heard.

Yesterday,
I learnt to bisect words,
Like we bisected triangles in maths class;
Splitting them from the middle,
Like Pinocchio noses,
And twisted promises.
I bisected 'd e m o c r a c y',
But was left with nothing but dust.

Yesterday, I felt each vein across my hand,
Screaming at me,
To not write that tweet,
To not publish that article,
To not be left at the mercy,
Of the shadows in our country.

Yesterday,
I learnt that as much as I scream and yell,
They can mute me,
With a flick of a finger.
I learnt that no one is voiceless.
They are either deliberately silenced,
Or preferably unheard.

Yesterday,
I learnt that if I talk
I have to be prepared,
To be hurt.
That if I scream,
I have to be prepared of the bars they put me behind.

Today,
I realise,
That my voice,
Is a weapon.
That each word I say,

Is being heard.

That yesterday,
Is fading.
And my voice,
Will always remain a weapon.

~Srina

A Sword and a Pen

A sword can wound your skin,
It can make you bleed,
But the pain is hollow,
A meaningless hurting.
A pen,
Can cut open your heart,
Each into a piece for the words engraved.
It can breathe through the paper,
And burn through the words.

The wounds will heal,
They aren't permanent,
But ink is.
What's once written,
Is never forgotten.

The soldiers might have fought,
But true strength lay in those vulnerable writers,
Who raised their voices,
But not their hands,
Who screamed through their words,
Not their weapons,
Who fought with a million others,
Through a mere newspaper,
And a mere word.

Righteous is he,
Who seeks justice by giving birth,
Not by killing,
For blood never gives birth,
Thoughts do.
Blood never saves,
It stains.

A sword may be sharp,
But each drop of blood collected on its tip,
Each person lost to pursue its shallow peace,
Makes the justice sought,
Simply not worth it.

The pen may be blunt,
But when a writer holds it between his aching fingers,
When the thoughts pour out of his mind,
They may set fire to the pages,
They may set fire to the world.

A sword kills,
But for a new world,
We need birth,
We need a womb in our mind,
And like a mother,
We need to nurture each bead of thought,

And each path,
Towards a new world.

For we don't need more blood in this world,
We need ink.
We don't need a sword to seek our pretense justice,
We need a thought,
We need a birth,
We need a pen.

~Srina

Women's Day

I wish today wasn't just a Whatsapp forward,
Not just a shallow pit of words,
Trying to make up for the rest of the three-sixty-
four days.

I wish, today,
We remember all the forgotten women,
No—not Marie Curie or Sania Mirza;
Not the ones whose name is engraved in our
history books,
But the ones,
We don't speak about.

I wish today, we remember,
All the Mothers and Sisters,
Who built bridges out of spears,
And shields out of tears,
Who have been ashamed forever,
Of the tragedy at the meeting of their thighs.

Who mopped floors,
Cooked food,
Gave birth to children,
And fulfilled,
The inevitable duty of a woman,
By crushing their own potential.

Who died with kitchen ceilings being their skies,
And a Husband's words their horizon.

They died with wings that never got the chance to fly,
But had always been fluttering.

Their remains lie not in the Whatsapp forwards,
But in the drains they cleaned,
The meals they fed,
And the kitchen they never left,
As they belong nowhere else.

They lie in the dowry papers stacked neatly in their drawer,
The *sindoor* they wore every day,
To carry the weight of their marriage,
Onto their forehead of broken dreams.

They lie in the misogynistic jokes cracked in dinner tables conversations,
And the ashes behind our history textbooks.

Today,
I wish not to remember the already recognized,
Not to remember the Mary Kom's or Marie Curie's,
I wish to remember the forgotten heroes,
The forgotten women,
Who still exist within each of us.

~*Srina*

The Ride Home

// Girl's perspective //

It's 12:06 a.m.,
Each second that passes,
A second I am at more risk,
My suit is full length, reaching my ankle,
Ma's hand sewn dupatta draped across my chest,
Yet, why is it that clothes have never made me feel safe?

I call an Auto,
An elderly Auto driver sitting in it,
Too old to hurt me,
Yet, old men are the ones who say it's always the girl's fault.
I watch his eyes in the rear window,
Making sure they are straight ahead, and not on me,
As the sin has always been mine,
The sin in between my thighs.

I tell him "Sarita Vihar",
And watch his wrinkled hands gently guide the wheel,
I notice his breaths are synchronised,

To the beat of the auto on the road,
And how he never locks eyes with me.

I have my phone in hand,
Papa's number on the screen,
Just in case something goes wrong,
Just in case I see a spark in his eyes that doesn't belong.

We reach my house,
It's dark outside.
Then he turns back to see me in the eyes for the first time,
As if examining me,
I see his age lingering in every little wrinkle across his face,
But age never brought trust.
I look around,
Is he waiting for his friends?
Is he looking for a weapon?
My breaths shorten,
And beads of sweat drip down my arms,
But the worst doesn't always happen,
And in a frail voice, the Auto driver says,
"Child, it's late, should I drop you inside?"

*

// Auto driver's perspective //

I think of my daughter when I see this girl,
How she feels afraid to go to college,
How my wife tells her to come home by 8 p.m.,
And the rage I feel when on a street, a boy whistles at her.

I see pieces of all the women I have known,
In this girl whose very name I don't know.

It's sad,
How even after thirty years of rotating this wheel,
And having two daughters of my own,
In the eyes of a girl out late,
I still have the potential to hurt them.

I know this girl looks for a reason to call the number she has open on her phone screen,
I know she is searching for reasons I am not to be trusted,
And honestly, after all I've seen in this country,
I don't expect to be trusted.

When I reach her destination: Sarita Vihar,
I notice not a single security guard on the gate,
Not a single piece of reassurance for this girl.

So I stop, count my breaths and gather every bit of courage in myself,
As the fear of being accused of a crime a man hasn't committed,
Is equal to the fear a girl feels around a man.

I see the fear in her eyes,
And gently say,
"Child, it's late. Should I drop you inside?"
And just for a fleeting moment,
I see her eyes reflecting,
Not a monster about to hurt her,
But a human willing to help.

~Srina

Beauty in Blood

You saw art in my blood,
Beauty in each slit etched onto me,
You saw your Ma's lipstick shade in the red,
The Gulmohar tree we sat under in the scarlet,
The beams of the glimmering sun in the orange,
And the dirt between your nails in the mustard.

You saw art in my blood,
Paintings spilling out of every edge of my skin,
And sculptures of all the broken things that reside within.

You saw museums,
And considered each scar as an artifact,
And each drop of blood,
Holy.

You saw through my wounds,
And saw not death pouring out,
But a painting,
A canvas,
To etch my own story onto,
To not let the darkness of yesterday,
Define the art I emit today.

You saw love pulsing in my hollow eyes,
And a world growing in the palm of my hands.
You saw beauty in the slits of my wrist,
You saw art in my pain,
Oh honey,
You saw beauty in my blood.

~Srina

Jar of Hearts

I never notice it,
But wherever I go, I carry a jar,
Not of pills,
But memories,
And paper cranes.

And on nights I am falling apart,
I unfold these cranes,
And watch them flutter to the breeze.

I think of Ma reading out Wizard of Oz,
My head resting on her lap,
Watching her voice paint images onto the air,
Images that the books I read now,
Can never seem to replicate.

I think of midsummer evenings on the Dhakuria terrace,
Plucking mangoes off the branches,
Dada would tell me every little detail about them,
Which was Dasheri, and which Chausa,
But for my young heart,
Who carefully planted this moment into the jar of hearts,
It was all the same.

I think of our Epsom home,
A home for three weeks,
Yet still a home.
A home which had a zebra striped sofa,
A home with a large silver oven,
A home with the smell of fresh cupcakes each night,
A temporary home,
Yet still one in the jar of hearts.

On nights I've hurt enough,
I stumble back onto the Rajaji national park,
I think of those incidents,
The paneer that melted on my tongue,
And the riverbed that sang under my feet,
I think of those moments now incorporated in every dinner table conversation,
To make up for the emptiness of today.

On nights I feel like nothing but a speck of dust,
I think of the books I sobbed while reading.
Books that made me stop,
Grab a pen,
Write a poem,
And sob some more.

I think of the feelings a mere word can give birth to.

I think of the first poem I ever wrote,
A raw piece of writing,
Un-polished and un-heard,
Yet I remember the feeling of accomplishment that hugged me,
A feeling that my hands weren't killers,
But creators.
I think of the realisation that crossed my mind,
That I had a power not possessed by everyone,
And that was the power to give birth to words.

I think of school,
The pang in my chest,
From being told to stand in the corridor outside for the first time,
And the thudding of my heart from bunking class the last time.

I think of the smell of books that I tried to bottle up and preserve,
But always managed to escape,
Just like all good things do.

I think of my first ever memory,
Which was falling on that brown staircase in Kaka's house,
Wearing shoes that clearly didn't belong to me,
And hitting my head onto the cement ground,
And letting out a tear-stained laugh.

I think of how my first ever memory was of falling,
Not happy smiles or blue skies,
But falling.

It's the irony of life,
How I have been learning to pick myself up, ever since.

~Srina

An Ode To The Writer I Once Was

You are a child,
A child who's abandoned and left alone,
Holding onto those crinkled pages,
As they are all that's left,
And waiting for your voice to echo,
To the people who silenced you.

You are a child,
Your words—half polished,
Trying to get themselves heard,
Yet too childish for us to take them to heart,
For the heart,
Has no place for nursery rhymes to rest.

You are a child,
Learning to walk,
But you still have mountains to climb,
And oceans to swim,
As each barrier you meet,
The more pain you'll have left to spin to gold.

You are just a child,
And sometimes I think poetry isn't for you,
For you are girl who draws sunflowers during art
class,
The child who sings to the stars,

Whose tender fingers aren't meant to be scraped,
And allowed to bleed—
Bleed through the same crayons you once drew sunflowers with.

You are a sponge,
You absorb new words,
From your Ma's cookbook,
And your favourite 2. P.M airing T.V show.
You take it all in,
And spill it onto the page,
With an occasional google search or two.

You're a particle of sand,
Who despite being so young and small,
Tries to imitate the oceans that brush upon you,
Only to leave your words shallow in contrast.

Watching you is like watching a child
sip *nimbu paani*,
While I chug whiskey.
It's like flipping through a slam book with all my crush's names,
After I had an arranged marriage,
It's like watching a kid blow bubbles with their spit,
While I smoke a cigarette.
It's the innocence that I can never quite get back.

Now I see you again,
You are eternities away from the first poem you wrote,
And acres away from that first draft.
You are beautifully broken.
You're a sunflower with grey petals now,
Yes you are still the same light hearted girl you once were.
Yes, your cheeks are still as rosy,
And your smile still as infectious,
But after all those years you taught yourself to walk,
Each page you ripped,
Each backspace key you clicked,
Each all-nighter you spent,
Just to breathe life into your work,
After all those times,
You grew.

No, you didn't grow peonies through the corners of your smile,
Or strands of gold from your hair,
You grew shields out of your pain.

And maybe,
When I now go through all those hidden diaries,
And the un-published poems,
I realise you are still a child,
But a child who can speak,

Who still falls down and stutters sometimes,
But she knows what she has on her mind,
She knows that her power lies not in the masks she wears,
But her voice,
That her voice lies not in the velvet sound she makes,
But in the words she bleeds.

I don't want to admit it,
But here in the solace of my pages I will,
You are the very first trace of me.
You are that first particle of sand,
That slowly multiplied after each tear,
To build the sand castle I weep in each night.

Your words became a womb to me and my work,
The me,
Who is writing this poem right now,
The me,
Who stills infringes your privacy by reading your first poems,
The me,
Who rose from those un-polished words,
And the me,
Who will always be thankful to the writer I once used to be.

~*Srina*

A Poet's Tragedy

Empty pages,
Scattered notebooks,
And scratched over lines.
Blotted ink,
With tears fading the crevices,
And bleeding words,
That stain everything he touches.

Isn't it sad?
A poet's tragedy?
How he,
Who finds meaning,
In every leaf he sees,
And every pebble he flicks,
Fails to find one,
In his own self?

~Srina

Acknowledgments

I'd like to thank my grandparents for their constant support and encouragement. I remember when I wrote my first poem, I showed it to them and despite it being childish—not once did they criticize me. Their encouragement was something so subtle at the time, just a pat on the back and a few kind words, but honestly, that made all the difference.

My Grandfather was the one who first planted the idea of publishing a book within my mind. He was the one who constantly nudged me for a manuscript—something that seemed annoying at first but has finally led to this.

Next, I'd like to thank my Parents. It is because of them that most of my thoughts are the way they are. Thank you for all the support. I know I'm not good at expressing it, but I'm grateful for you both.

And also, huge thanks to my Sister, whose creative and artistic talent have made the cover design of this book possible. She has always been the silent motivator in the family. She is the one who has exposed me to so many new ideas and perceptions. Yes, she did teach me science to pass my exams but she also taught me what capitalism, socialism, fascism and the flaws in society were. Many of my thoughts have been inspired by her liberal ideas.

And finally, thank you to all the artists out there, unrecognized and unnoticed, who create art every single day—they are the ones who inspire me to keep writing.

About the author

Srina Bose is a thirteen-year-old poet living in New Delhi with strong family connections in Kolkata. This collection of poems was written in 2020 amidst the scourge of the global pandemic. Srina considers poetry as a medium to express and vent. Besides writing, she enjoys debating and elocution and has also taken part in several short movies and plays. This is her second collection of poems.

About the book

When you try so hard to find light amongst the darkness,
You're ready to believe the light never even existed,
That the pain is all that is yours,
And that death is what breathes life into you.

She has always been told that there is a light at the end of the tunnel. This book is a journey towards that. But what if her horizons have faded away? What if the light that was meant to guide her out—simply a matchstick blown away by the wind? It's the search for the roses in her mind—the beauty in the pain, and a happy ending in a eulogy. It's the painstaking journey towards a new self. The heartache, the disease and finally the revival that gives her a chance to complete the story she once started.

'Roses In My Mind' is the perfect blend of all the flawed emotions that make us human.

www.ingramcontent.com/pod-product-compliance
Ingram Content Group UK Ltd.
Pitfield, Milton Keynes, MK11 3LW, UK
UKHW021647190726
13853UKWH00001B/117